GROWING GIFTS

INTRODUCTION BY RODDY LLEWELLYN

This book was a lot of fun to write, and I hope that an equal amount of pleasure will be derived by readers who are keen to grow gifts.

I am grateful that I have been given the opportunity to introduce children and amateur gardeners alike to the wonders of Mother Nature's Kingdom. My introduction to gardening happened when I was three with a packet of nasturtium seeds. I will never forget those first shoots coming up through the soil. The fact that they continued to grow, producing first leaves and then flowers, struck me then, as it still does now, as being nothing short of miraculous.

I am now watching my own children discover the magic. I shall always remember the expression on the face of Rosie aged four, pulling up her first carrot, after the long and exciting wait since she sowed the seed months before. I like to think that such memories will stay with her for life, to pass on to her children.

Much pleasure can be gained by growing your own gifts, because growing a gift is a perfect way of enabling you to give something special to someone special.

Roderic Llewellyn

Chapmans Publishers Ltd
141-143 Drury Lane
London WC2B 5TB

A CIP catalogue record for this book
is available from the British Library

ISBN 1 85592 608 3

First published by Chapmans 1992

Copyright © Roderic Llewellyn 1992

The right of Roderic Llewellyn to be identified as the author
of this work has been asserted by him in accordance with the
Copyright, Designs and Patents Act 1988.

Designed by Bill Craig (with thanks to Chris Hazelwood)

Cover photograph by D. Bentley
courtesy of FLOWERS of Sevenoaks

Inside photographs by Heather Angel

Typeset by Pica Rule of Sevenoaks
Produced in Great Britain by S B Print & Design Ltd

GROWING GIFTS

Roddy Llewellyn

CHAPMANS

January

PLANT/FLOWER	WITCH HAZEL
WHAT IT GROWS FROM	It is easiest to grow a witch hazel tree from a small bought plant.
WHEN TO PLANT	October.
WHERE TO PLANT	Outside in a large container or in the garden, in either case where it receives plenty of sunshine.
HOW DEEP TO PLANT	Plant the same depth as it was in its container.
IN WHAT SORT OF SOIL	Plant in Levington peat-based potting compost, with some well-rotted organic matter at the bottom of the pot.
WHAT YOU NEED	One large pot, minimum 2 feet in diameter (about 60cm), one bag of Levington compost, small stones or broken crocks, watering can, bone meal, sharp knife, and a small amount of well-rotted organic matter.
HOW TO PLANT	First put in small stones or broken crocks for drainage so that all drainage holes are covered. Next put a few handfuls of well-rotted organic matter in the bottom of the pot, then half-fill the pot with potting compost and firm it down. Place the plant in its container in the centre of the large pot on the compost, fill in around it and firm. Gently remove the plant and you will have left behind a moulded shape. Into this scatter some bonemeal sparingly. You may have to add more compost so that the base of the plant is 3 inches (8cm) below the brim of the pot. 
AFTERCARE	So long as you feed your tree adequately you will not have to change the compost or repot for several years. A top dressing of fresh compost every spring is a good idea, having first scraped away the top 2 or 3 inches (5-8cm) of old compost. In severe winters the pot will have to be protected with something similar to 'bubbly plastic' to prevent frost getting into the sides of the pot and damaging the roots.
WATERING	Water thoroughly immediately after planting. You will not have to water during the winter as the plant is outside, but you will have to during the summer, especially during hot, dry spells.
FEEDING	Use a liquid feed once a month.
GIFT IDEAS	Their lovely scented yellow flowers last well. Present a single stem of witch hazel in its own vase. Or wrap cotton wool round the cut end of a single stem, then wrap with kitchen foil and ribbon.

ALGERIAN IRIS	BEGONIA REX†
A thick wiry root (a 'rhizome').	Leaf cutting. †Parental supervision required.
September.	June.
In an outside pot or window box, or a warm, sunny part of the garden.	In a pot, in a light, warm indoor room, out of direct sunlight.
Lay it flat just below the soil surface.	Leaves are laid on the surface of the soil.
Poor. It does not like a rich soil. John Innes No 1 is ideal for pots.	Any multi-purpose potting compost.
A 6-inch (15cm) pot, a root, a small bag of John Innes No 1 compost, a stone and gravel for drainage.	A flower pot, one small bag of cutting compost, sharp knife, polythene bag, rubber band, small watering can, small stones and a saucer.
First put a stone over the drainage hole, then a handful of gravel in the bottom of the pot, then three-quarters fill with compost and firm with your fingertips. Lay root (one per a 6-inch/15cm pot) on the surface. Sprinkle compost over the root so that it is just covered.	Make sure that your flower pot is wide enough to accommodate the leaf. Fill it with cutting compost and firm it down with the tips of your fingers, then water it well. Cut a leaf off an existing plant, leaving 1-2 inches (2½-5cm) of stalk, turn it upside-down, and cut main veins in four or five places with sharp knife. Lay the leaf face upwards on the cutting compost, weighing it down with the small stones. Secure the polythene bag over the top of the pot with the rubber band, making one or two small holes for ventilation and place the pot on a saucer in a light place out of direct sunlight.
They live out of doors where they thrive on neglect!	A rooted plantlet will start to grow at some or all of the places where the leaf was cut. Once these have grown a couple of inches in height, they can be potted on with a general compost into 3-inch wide (8cm) pots. Begonias like a moderate temperature (max 21°C/70°F; min 12°C/54°F).
Little and often when coming into flower, otherwise not necessary.	Keep compost just moist at all times during summer, but reduce watering in the winter.
Not necessary.	Every 2 weeks from April-September with a liquid feed.
Flowers vary from dark to light blue. They make excellent cut flowers as they last for so long in a vase or jam jar. Tie with a ribbon.	These are easy houseplants to grow. They put up with a lot of abuse! Give an established plant with its pot wrapped in gift paper and ribbon.

February

PLANT/FLOWER	SNOWDROPS†
WHAT IT GROWS FROM	A bulb. †Parental supervision required.
WHEN TO PLANT	October.
WHERE TO PLANT	In a window box, flower pot or out in the garden.
HOW DEEP TO PLANT	2 inches (5cm).
IN WHAT SORT OF SOIL	Any multi-purpose potting compost.
WHAT YOU NEED	Window box, small stones, fork and trowel, compost and bulbs.
HOW TO PLANT	First secure the window box on to a strong, deep window ledge. A child will have to get a grown-up to help with this. Then spread a couple of handfuls of stones along the bottom. Fill with compost and firm. Using the trowel, plant the bulbs the right way up, and rake over with the fork to make the compost level.
AFTERCARE	A top dressing of fresh compost every spring.
WATERING	Regularly during the summer, at least every other day.
FEEDING	A foliar feed immediately after flowering.
GIFT IDEAS	Wrap cut ends of snowdrops in damp cotton wool and lay flowers in a small basket lined with moss or hay from the pet shop. Or pull snowdrop flowers (as opposed to cutting them) so that their stalks are long, until you have a nice bunch. Wrap their ends in damp cotton wool, kitchen foil and ribbon.

DAFFODILS	**CLIVIA**
A bulb.	A side shoot.
October to December.	April.
In a bowl. If grown outside in the garden or in a window box they will flower in April.	In a pot indoors.
4 inches (10cm).	Plant side shoots so that all roots are below soil surface.
Any multi-purpose potting compost.	Loam-based potting compost.
A ceramic or terracotta bowl, daffodil bulbs, stone, gravel, potting compost.	A side shoot, a 6-inch diameter (15cm) flower pot, compost, a saucer and some small stones.
First put a stone over the drainage hole, then a handful of gravel into the bottom of the bowl and then half-fill it with compost. Firm the compost with your fingertips, stroke it level and lay the bulbs gently on to the compost. Make sure they are the right way up, and just cover them with compost.	First put a handful of small stones in the bottom of the pot. Then fill it to the brim with compost and firm it down with your fingertips, so that it lies 1 inch (2½cm) below the rim of the pot. Using your index finger make a hole large enough to accommodate the roots. Stick the roots of the plant in, firm and water thoroughly.
Put potted bulbs in a dark and cool place for 8-10 weeks, keeping the compost moist at all times. When the shoots are about 1 inch (2½cm) high the bowls can be brought into a light, but still cool place. Once the plants have reached a height of about 4 inches (10cm), they can be brought into the house, and this is the time when they make superb gifts. After flowering, cut off the dead flower, and plant the bulbs, complete with leaves and flower stalks, outside in the garden, 6 inches (15cm) deep.	Clivias are happy in ordinary room temperatures, and prefer it cool during autumn and winter (10-15°C/50-59°F). Place pot on a saucer. Do not repot until the plant is really pot-bound as it flowers better when its roots are restricted.
Water thoroughly immediately after planting, and keep compost moist at all times thereafter.	Keep compost moist from March to September, but water sparingly during winter.
Use a foliar feed immediately after flowering.	Once or twice a month with a liquid feed from March to September.
Daffodils can also be grown in ordinary flower pots indoors. Smaller bulbs of dwarf daffodil species need to be planted 3 inches (8cm) deep. For giving, make sure your bowl is pretty.	Clivias can also be propagated from seed. Many other plants can be grown from side shoots. If the bowl is plain stick some silk flowers on the side.

March

PLANT/FLOWER	MUSTARD AND CRESS
WHAT IT GROWS FROM	Seed.
WHEN TO PLANT	February.
WHERE TO PLANT	In a used margarine/yoghurt carton.
HOW DEEP TO PLANT	Lay seed on surface.
IN WHAT SORT OF SOIL	Kitchen paper.
WHAT YOU NEED	A used margarine/yoghurt carton, kitchen paper and seed.
HOW TO PLANT	Line the base of the carton with kitchen paper, moisten it, and then scatter seed thickly over it, one seed deep. 
AFTERCARE	Start off in a warm, dark place like an airing cupboard then keep in a warm room.
WATERING	Keep kitchen paper wet at all times.
FEEDING	Not necessary.
GIFT IDEAS	Cut with a pair of scissors as and when needed as additions to sandwiches and salads. Also useful as garnish. If you are giving the carton, paint with enamel paint to any design of your choice.

AFRICAN VIOLET†

Leaf cuttings.
†Parental supervision required.

Midsummer.

Indoors, in a 3-inch (8cm) pot.

Insert leaf stalk into potting compost.

Any multi-purpose potting compost.

Two 3-inch (8cm) pots, compost, a saucer, polythene bag, a few stones, a rubber band and a sharp stick.

First place a few stones in the bottom of the pot, followed by compost which should be firmed in with the tips of your fingers. Cut a healthy leaf, with 2 inches (5cm) of stalk, from another plant and put it, stalk first, into the compost. Water, and cover in a polythene bag, with a couple of holes for ventilation, secured with a rubber band.

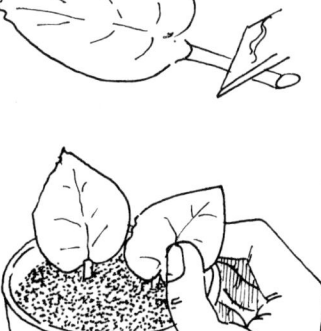

Once the fresh young leaves which start growing at the base of the parent leaf form a new plant, it should be repotted into another 3-inch (8cm) pot containing moisture-retentive compost. It will be happiest in the warm, humid conditions of the greenhouse. If grown indoors, therefore, place the pot on a large saucer of gravel and water. Keep shaded during the summer, and on a sunny windowsill during winter.

Water carefully, making sure that water does not splash the leaves. Reduce watering in winter.

Feed with diluted tomato fertiliser to promote flowering.

African violets are well suited to a terrarium which makes a very special gift. If in a pot, wrap with crepe paper and ribbon.

PRICKLY CACTI

Seed.

April.

Indoors in a 6-inch (15cm) pot.

Surface sown, and cover lightly with sifted compost.

Cactus compost.

6-inch (15cm) pot, cactus compost, cactus seed, polythene bag and a rubber band.

Sprinkle seed on compost surface and cover lightly with sifted compost. Water, cover with polythene bag secured with a rubber band, and keep warm (18-21°C/65-70°F).

Be patient for seed to germinate! Some seed will start to germinate 3 weeks after sowing and others several weeks after that! Young plantlets can be potted on into their own 3-inch (8cm) pots once they are established. Cacti enjoy sitting in sunny windows.

Keep the compost just moist in the seed tray. Once the plants become established, they can be watered regularly during the summer, but hardly at all during the winter.

Start feeding during their second year with a weak solution of liquid feed, once a year during early summer.

There is a huge range of cacti to experiment with. Paint the pot with enamel paint so that it really stands out on the windowsill.

April

PLANT/FLOWER	CROCUS
WHAT IT GROWS FROM	A bulb.
WHEN TO PLANT	Autumn.
WHERE TO PLANT	In a 6-inch (15cm) pot.
HOW DEEP TO PLANT	2 inches (5cm).
IN WHAT SORT OF SOIL	Multi-purpose potting compost.
WHAT YOU NEED	12 crocus bulbs, small stones, 6-inch (15cm) pot, compost, piece of black polythene and string.
HOW TO PLANT	Put a handful of stones in the bottom of the pot, fill it with compost, and firm with your fingertips. Gently place the bulbs in the compost and just cover. Cover the pot in black polythene secured around the pot with string.

AFTERCARE	Leave in a cool (but not freezing) place for 8 or 9 weeks. After this time the bulbs can be exposed to light, but must be kept cool (about 10°C/50°F) until buds are well formed, after which time they can be brought indoors. After flowering they can be planted out in the garden.
WATERING	During their cool period they will hardly need to be watered at all. However, once in the warmth of indoors their compost must not be allowed to dry out.
FEEDING	Foliar feed immediately after flowering.
GIFT IDEAS	Bulbs forced indoors will not flower again unless they are planted outside. Put the pot you are giving in a wicker basket the same size.

PRIMROSE	**AMARYLLIS (Hippeastrum)**
Seed.	A bulb.
March.	March.
Initially seed tray, then 3-inch (8cm) pots or out in the garden.	In a 6-inch (15cm) pot, indoors, on a sunny windowsill.
Very shallow.	Leave the top half of the bulb uncovered.
Multi-purpose compost.	Multi-purpose potting compost.
Primrose seed, seed tray, compost.	Multi-purpose potting compost, 6-inch (15cm) pot, one amaryllis bulb, small stones.
Sprinkle seed thinly on top of compost in a seed tray, and cover with polythene secured with string. 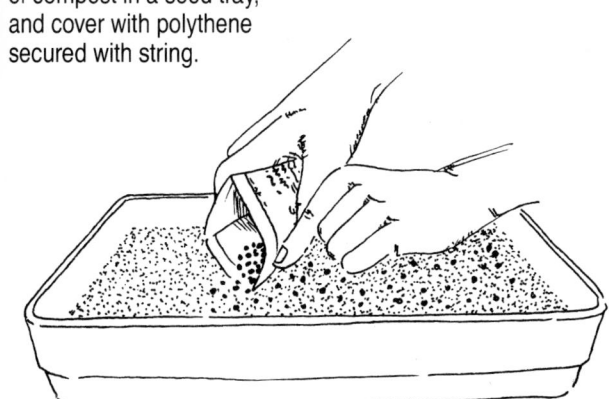	First put a handful of small stones in the bottom of the pot, followed by the potting compost. Firm the compost with your fingertips so that the pot is three-quarters full. Gently place the large bulb on the compost surface and fill in around it so that it is half-covered only. Water. 
Keep just moist. As soon as the seedlings appear remove the polythene. Keep them in a sheltered and shaded place where there is plenty of air circulating. Pot on individual plants, by lifting them by their leaves and *not* their stems, using the same compost. Keep young plants outside in a light place where they will not be baked by the midday sun.	Keep the plant at a temperature of 16-21°C/61-70°F during spring and summer, and 10-12°C/50-54°F when the bulb is resting during the winter. Top dress every year, and repot every three.
Water regularly so that the compost is kept moist at all times.	Keep compost moist until the foliage dies down in September/October, afterwards let the compost dry out until the bulb starts into growth again.
A 'thank you' feed with a liquid feed during and after flowering.	Feed every 2 weeks after the plant has flowered until the autumn, when the foliage starts to die down.
Polyanthuses, more colourful 'primroses', are grown in the same way. Flowering plants can have dried flowers stuck on their pots, either singly, in groups, or all over.	Wrap the pot with a pretty piece of old material and secure it with a ribbon.

May

PLANT/FLOWER	BLUEBELLS
WHAT IT GROWS FROM	A bulb.
WHEN TO PLANT	Autumn.
WHERE TO PLANT	Outside in a pot or window box, or out in the garden.
HOW DEEP TO PLANT	3 inches (8cm).
IN WHAT SORT OF SOIL	Ordinary potting compost.
WHAT YOU NEED	Bulbs, compost, 6-inch pot (15cm), small stones.
HOW TO PLANT	Put a handful of small stones in the bottom of the pot, then add compost, firming it with your fingertips. Gently place the bulbs on the compost and cover to a depth of 3 inches (8cm).  
AFTERCARE	None required.
WATERING	None required unless the weather is dry and/or windy. If so the pots should be watered, otherwise Mother Nature will see to it!
FEEDING	Feed immediately after flowering with a foliar feed.
GIFT IDEAS	Bluebells are normally grown outside in the garden. Wrap pot in kitchen foil or paint it white with enamel paint.

BASIL (Sweet)	COLEUS
Seed.	Seed.
Early April.	February.
In a 6-inch (15cm) pot.	Seed tray or pot, indoors.
Half an inch (1cm).	Very shallow.
Ordinary potting compost.	Seed compost.
Seed, 6-inch (15cm) pots, compost, a handful of small stones or gravel.	Seed, seed compost, seed tray.
Put a handful of small stones or gravel into the bottom of the pot and then fill with compost. Firm. Sow two seeds in the centre of the pot. Put in a warm room in the light, somewhere like the kitchen windowsill.	Sprinkle seed finely onto compost in seed tray and water. Keep at temperature of 15-18°C (60-65°F) while seeds are germinating. Then pot on plants into individual 3-inch (8cm) pots as gifts.
Pull out the weaker plant and discard. Pick out the shoot tips regularly and pick off flowers.	Keep plants warm, moist and shaded from hottest sunlight. You can keep them outside during the summer. Pinch out flower heads as they appear — if they are allowed to flower the colourful leaves will suffer. Pinch back long shoots to keep the plant bushy.
Keep compost moist at all times.	Keep moist.
Not necessary.	Every 2 weeks from April-September with a liquid feed.
Sow a second batch in September for winter use. Wrap pot in gift wrapping paper secured with a ribbon tied in a bow.	Very easily grown from cuttings in August. Present your coleus in a terracotta pot smothered in shells on plaster of Paris.

June

PLANT/FLOWER	MINIATURE ROSES
WHAT IT GROWS FROM	A bought plant.
WHEN TO PLANT	May.
WHERE TO PLANT	In a pot — minimum 9 inches (23cm), outside, or planted directly into the garden.
HOW DEEP TO PLANT	The same depth as the bought plant.
IN WHAT SORT OF SOIL	Any multi-purpose potting compost.
WHAT YOU NEED	One miniature rose plant, a 9-inch (23cm) pot, a handful of stones and some compost.
HOW TO PLANT	Put a handful of small stones in the bottom of the pot followed by a handful of compost. Remove plant from existing pot and place it centrally in the new pot. Fill in with compost around the root mould firming as you go with the tips of your fingers. The base of the plant should be 1 inch (2½cm) below the soil level of the pot. Water.

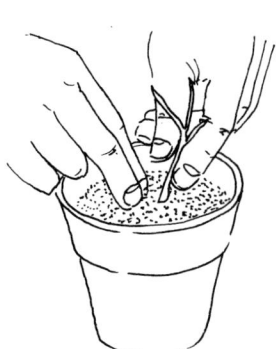

AFTERCARE	Easier to keep outside. Remove deadheads after flowering.
WATERING	Keep moist at all times, and do not allow it to dry out in summer.
FEEDING	Liquid feed every 2 weeks.
GIFT IDEAS	It is always a good idea to repot your miniature rose after you have brought it home. Present in a wicker basket (the same size as the pot) with a ribbon around it, tied in a bow.

SWEET PEAS†	GERANIUMS†
Seed. †Parental assistance required.	Cuttings. †Parental supervision required.
February/March.	August/September.
Outdoors in large pots, or flowering positions in gardens.	In 3-inch (8cm) pots.
2 inches (5cm).	Insert cuttings 1 inch (2½cm) into compost.
Multi-purpose potting compost with fertiliser added if planting in a pot, and deeply dug, rich soil, if planting out in the garden.	Any multi-purpose potting compost.
One large pot (min. 14 inches/35cm) or half-barrel, seeds, 6 six-foot bamboo canes, string and gravel.	A pair of scissors, an existing geranium plant, 3-inch (8cm) pot, compost and a handful of gravel or small stones.
If a large pot, put a stone over drainage hole. Put 2 inches (5cm) of gravel in the base of the container, and then fill it with the compost. Plant 2 seeds every 8 inches (20cm) apart, inserting a bamboo cane at each station 6 inches (15cm) deep. Once completed, bunch the tops of the canes together with a piece of string. 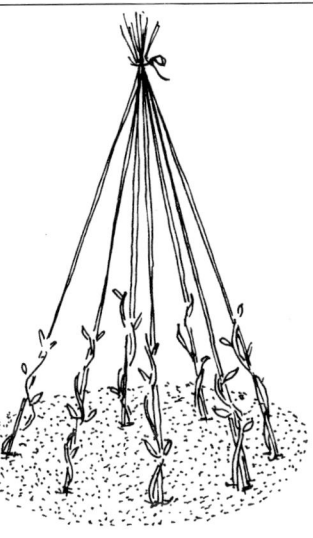	First put 1 inch (2½cm) of small stones or gravel in the bottom of the pot, followed by compost to the brim. Firm compost with the tips of your fingers. Cut a 6-inch (15cm) shoot from an existing geranium plant, cutting through a leaf joint. Remove the lower leaves and any flower buds, and insert the cutting 1 inch (2½cm) into the compost. Water thoroughly. (Do *not* use a rooting hormone.) 
Keep plants tied to canes as they grow.	To begin with keep your cutting in a well-lit place, but out of direct sunlight. After 3 weeks it will have developed roots, and can be introduced to more light. In winter keep your plant on a sunny windowsill at about 15°C/60°F.
Keep compost moist.	Keep well watered until autumn when watering is slowly reduced to a minimum until warmer weather returns in the spring.
Liquid feed every 2 weeks once they have started to produce flower buds.	A liquid feed every 2 weeks in spring to encourage new foliage.
Never allow plants to form seed heads. If you do, the plants will die. Present a bunch, ends wrapped in damp cotton wool covered in kitchen foil and tied in a beautiful ribbon.	Present in a pot smothered in shells pressed into plaster of Paris.

July

PLANT/FLOWER	STRAWBERRIES
WHAT IT GROWS FROM	A bought plant or runners from a friend's plant.
WHEN TO PLANT	Spring.
WHERE TO PLANT	In a growbag, in individual pots, in a 'strawberry barrel' or out in the garden.
HOW DEEP TO PLANT	Plant so that roots are in the compost.
IN WHAT SORT OF SOIL	A 'fertilised' growbag.
WHAT YOU NEED	One growbag, eight young plants.
HOW TO PLANT	Cut eight small crosses in the growbag equidistantly, and insert plants.

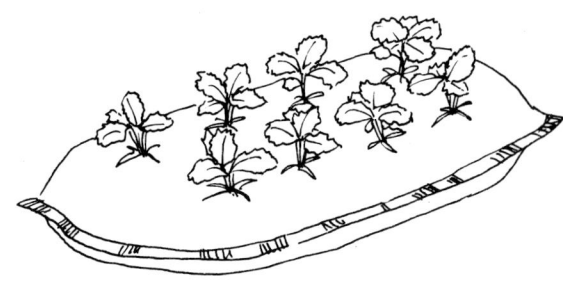

AFTERCARE	Strawberries need a lot of sunshine if they are to fruit well. Remove runners by pinching them out as they appear, unless they are needed as fresh stock. You are supposed to remove flowers from plants during their first season of growth to prevent them from fruiting, but if you want to you can leave 2 or 3 on each plant.
WATERING	Keep compost moist during growing season.
FEEDING	Use a tomato fertiliser only if leaves turn pale.
GIFT IDEAS	Also try alpine strawberries, which are smaller but tastier! Place in a basket lined with straw (available from pet shop) and tie a ribbon bow on the handle.

MORNING GLORY

Seed.

Late March/early April.

In a pot in a greenhouse or indoors.

Just lightly covered with soil.

General purpose potting compost.

3-inch (8cm) pots, seed, compost, and gravel or small stones.

First put a few small stones in the bottom of a 3-inch (8cm) pot and then fill it with compost. Firm it down with the tips of your fingers so that the top of the compost sits just below the rim of the pot. Soak the seed in water for 24 hours then plant one or two in the centre of each pot.

Keep them quite warm, at a minimum temperature of 13°C/55°F. A day or two in a warm place like an airing cupboard might help them to get started. Once established they will need a string or tall cane to wind themselves around. They can then be potted into a larger pot 8-inch (20cm) and kept in a sunny window or greenhouse, or be planted outside up against a sunny, south-facing wall.

Keep compost moist at all times.

Every 2 weeks with a liquid feed.

Morning Glory can also be grown outside in a sunny spot, allowed to scramble freely over shrubs. Give away when plant is 6 inches (15cm) high. Wrap pot in a pretty piece of material and tie with a ribbon.

LILY (Lilium candidum)

A bulb.

January/February.

In a 12-inch (30cm) pot.

Leave the nose of bulb just showing above the soil surface.

John Innes No 1, with a couple of handfuls of sharp sand added.

3 four-foot bamboo canes, 12-inch (30cm)pot, 3 bulbs of *Lilium candidum*, compost, a couple of handfuls of sharp sand (builder's sand will not do), stones or crocks.

First place stones or crocks in the bottom of the pot and then fill with compost. Plant bulbs and as you do so put in a bamboo stake between the bulbs and the edge of the pot for support when they grow tall.

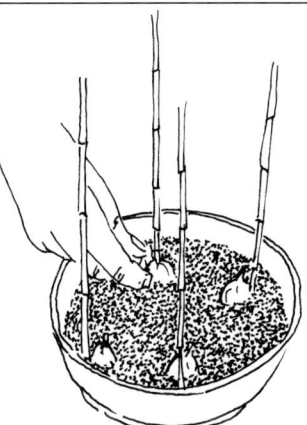

They can be left in the same pot for 3-4 years before dividing. Leave outside all the time except when you want to bring the pot indoors while the plants are flowering.

Keep compost moist during growing season.

Feed in April/May with a tomato fertiliser and cut off flower spikes as soon as they are finished.

Place moss on soil surface and tie a ribbon with a bow around the pot.

August

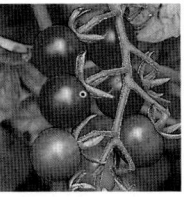

PLANT/FLOWER	CHERRY TOMATOES
WHAT IT GROWS FROM	Seed.
WHEN TO PLANT	March.
WHERE TO PLANT	In a seed tray.
HOW DEEP TO PLANT	Quarter of an inch ($\frac{1}{2}$cm).
IN WHAT SORT OF SOIL	Seed compost.
WHAT YOU NEED	Tomato seed, seed compost, seed tray, general compost, growbag, 2-foot canes.
HOW TO PLANT	Sprinkle seed onto seed tray containing seed compost, water thoroughly, and keep at a temperature of 20-25°C/68-78°F. When they are 1-2 inches (2.$\frac{1}{2}$-5cm) high, they are transplanted individually into 3-inch (8cm) pots, containing a general compost, at the same temperature. In May place young plants in a growbag or 12-inch (30cm) pot, with 2-foot (60cm) canes for support. Cut 3 small crosses equidistantly along the top of the growbag and insert the plants.
AFTERCARE	If not under glass, plants must be positioned in a sunny place on a balcony or in a garden where they are protected from the wind.
WATERING	Keep compost moist.
FEEDING	Every 2 weeks with a tomato fertiliser.
GIFT IDEAS	There are many different sorts of tomato to grow, but cherry tomatoes are rather special. Line a basket with straw, available from pet shops, and arrange tomatoes on top. Stick a clump of dried flowers to the rim of the basket and tie a ribbon bow around the handle. They are also wonderful with a party dip.

NASTURTIUM	**ROSEMARY**
Seed.	A bought plant.
April.	Spring or summer.
In a 6-inch (15cm) pot.	In a 6-inch (15cm) pot.
1 inch (2cm).	Replant at same depth as bought plant.
General compost.	John Innes No 1.
Seed, seed tray, compost.	6-inch (15cm) pot, a small bag of John Innes No 1, small stones or gravel and later on, scissors, string, airtight jar.
Once the seedlings have grown they can be planted outside in the garden or in a 12-inch (30cm) pot on a balcony, in a sunny position.	Put about ½ inch (1cm) of small stones into the bottom of the pot and then a couple of handfuls of compost. Place the plant into the pot and fill around and over rootball until soil is about ½ inch (1cm) below the rim of the pot, and firm with finger tips. Water thoroughly and stand out of direct sunshine for a few days.
Allow to scramble where they wish.	Your rosemary plant will have to be repotted every year to a new pot one size larger. It will eventually grow into quite a large plant.
Water every day. Keep a very close watch for blackfly and pick off infected leaves or shoots as soon as you see them.	Be careful not to overwater. Allow compost to dry out almost completely between waterings.
Every 2 weeks with a liquid feed.	Not necessary.
The flowers and leaves are delicious in a salad. Pick and arrange leaves *and* flowers in damp moss. Remember they must be eaten fresh.	Potted rosemary can overwinter in a cool greenhouse, but is just as happy to be left outside in a moist sheltered spot. Rosemary is cut and dried for winter use. Cut a dozen or so 6-inch (15cm) healthy shoots, and hang them up in a bunch tied with string in an airy place or spread them out in the sun to dry. They should have dried in about 3 weeks, then the shoots can be rubbed between the palms and dried and put into an airtight jar. Present dried rosemary in a jar with personalised label and a ribbon tied around the neck of the jar.

September

PLANT/FLOWER	TANGERINE
WHAT IT GROWS FROM	A pip.
WHEN TO PLANT	Spring.
WHERE TO PLANT	In a 3-inch (8cm) pot, in a warm, dark place.
HOW DEEP TO PLANT	1 inch (2½cm).
IN WHAT SORT OF SOIL	Ordinary potting compost.
WHAT YOU NEED	3-inch (8cm) pot, compost, clear plastic bag, string, and a handful of small stones or gravel.
HOW TO PLANT	First put 1 inch (2½cm) of gravel or small stones in the bottom of the pot, and then fill up with compost, and firm. Plant the pip, cover the top of the pot with a plastic bag, and keep in a warm cupboard.

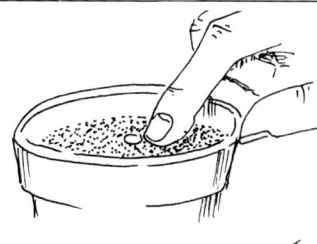

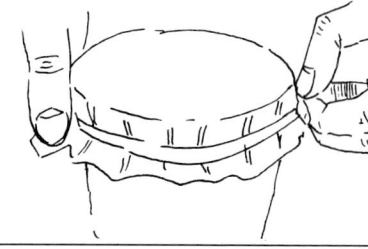

AFTERCARE	When the seedling is about 4 inches (10cm) tall, it is repotted, picking it up by its leaves and *not* by its stem, into a 6-inch (15cm) pot, and introduced to the light. Repot every year into pots one size larger. Minimum winter temperature 12°C/54°F. Keep outside during the summer if you can.
WATERING	Keep moist during summer but water sparsely during winter.
FEEDING	Once a month from April to September.
GIFT IDEAS	A citrus plant grown from a pip at home will seldom produce fruit of the parent plant. If you want a plant guaranteed to produce tangerines, oranges or lemons, you will have to spend a lot of money on an established fruiting plant. As a present, sprinkle colourful gravel on the soil surface, tie a ribbon around the pot and finish with a bow.

CHINESE LANTERNS	FUCHSIA
Seed.	Small plants are very inexpensive in the spring. Buy ones marked 'hardy'.
March.	Spring.
In a 6-inch (15cm) pot.	Pot on into 6-inch (15cm) pot using a multi-purpose potting compost when you get it home.
Just lightly cover with soil and gently firm down.	The same depth as the bought plant.
Seed compost.	Multi-purpose potting compost.
Seed, pot, compost.	Multi-purpose potting compost, 6-inch (15cm) pot, and a few small stones or gravel.
Sow about 10 seeds in the pot, and water. Select strongest plantlets to be potted on into individual 6-inch (15cm) pots. 	Place 1 inch (2½cm) of small stones or gravel in the bottom of a 6-inch (15cm) pot with a couple of inches of compost on top. Remove the plant from its original pot and place it in the new one, firming compost around the root ball as you go. 
In autumn pot on 3 plants into a 14-inch (35cm) pot. The flower stalks produced at the end of the following summer will need staking before they are picked and dried. This plant requires a sunny position out of doors.	Repot every year into a pot one size larger. Keep out of strong sunlight, especially during the middle of the day in summer. During the winter keep the plant in a cool room, or unheated conservatory.
Keep compost moist during growing season.	Don't overwater! Water little and often during the summer and reduce to a minimum in winter.
Once a month with a liquid feed if grown in a container. If grown out in the garden it should not need feeding at all.	Liquid feed, using a tomato fertiliser once a month from April to September.
Individual 'lanterns' can be sprayed silver and gold, and used as decorations on the Christmas tree. Otherwise, stems of lanterns are used in dried flower arrangements during the winter. Tie a ribbon with a bow around a bunch of dried Chinese lanterns.	Smother pot in sea shells on plaster of Paris.

October

PLANT/FLOWER	MINT
WHAT IT GROWS FROM	A root.
WHEN TO PLANT	September.
WHERE TO PLANT	Indoors in the warmth, in a 6-inch (15cm) pot.
HOW DEEP TO PLANT	1 inch (2½cm).
IN WHAT SORT OF SOIL	Any multi-purpose compost.
WHAT YOU NEED	6-inch (15cm) pot, compost, 4 inches long (10cm), plump mint roots, and a handful of small stones or gravel.
HOW TO PLANT	The best place to find mint roots is where mint is growing freely in the garden. Dig them up with a spade, shake off the soil and bring the roots indoors. On a chopping board cut off 4-inch (10cm) lengths, choosing the plumpest roots. Then put a handful of small stones or gravel in the bottom of the pot, and then three-quarters fill with compost, firming down with the tips of your fingers. Place the roots flat and cover so that the compost is 1 inch (2½cm) below the rim of the pot. Water.
AFTERCARE	Keep in a warm room on a sunny windowsill. Pinch out stem tips to encourage side shoots. Pinch out flower buds. Fresh roots will be needed every winter.
WATERING	Keep compost moist.
FEEDING	Not necessary.
GIFT IDEAS	Delicious fresh mint throughout the winter! A very special gift for mum's or a friend's roast lamb and garnish. Give a pot for the kitchen with a ribbon tied around it with a bow.

GIANT PUMPKINS	**GUERNSEY LILY (Nerine)**
Seed.	A bulb.
May.	July–September.
In a fertilised growbag (or out in the garden on a compost heap if you have one).	Outside in a window box or pot, or out in the garden.
1 inch (2½cm).	2½ inches (6cm).
If planted outside in the garden, in soil enriched with manure.	Ordinary potting compost.
Giant pumpkin seed, a growbag, 3-inch (8cm) pots (1 seed per pot), seed compost and a handful of small stones or gravel.	4 bulbs, one 8-inch (20cm) pot, compost and a handful of small stones or gravel.
First put a handful of small stones or gravel in the bottom of the pot and then fill it with the seed compost, firming it with your fingertips so that it is 1 inch (2½cm) below the rim of the pot. Insert the seed 1 inch (2½cm) deep and water thoroughly.	Put a handful of small stones or gravel in the bottom of the pot, and fill three-quarters full with the compost. Place the bulbs gently onto the compost and cover them about 2½ inches (6cm) deep (tips just below the surface).
Keep the young seedling warm in an average temperature of 18°C/65°F, and plant it outside once all threats of frost are over, in a place where it will receive plenty of sunshine. Plant 1 plant per growbag, otherwise 3 feet (1m) apart in the open garden.	Diamond lilies like growing in a hot sunny place. Lift and replant every 4 or 5 years. They thrive on neglect.
Keep compost in growbag moist at all times during the growing season. Water outdoor plants every day during dry weather.	Keep compost moist during dry spells in winter.
Feed every 2 weeks with a liquid feed during growing season.	Not necessary.
Grow your own or your friend's giant pumpkin for Hallowe'en! Hollow it out, carve out a face and light it within with a nightlight to ward off evil spirits! To get really big ones you must pick off all the new fruits after the first one or two have formed so that the plant puts all its effort into just a couple of pumpkins.	Tie a bunch with white ribbon, or give the pot painted with white enamel and tied with white ribbon.

November

PLANT/FLOWER	CYCLAMEN
WHAT IT GROWS FROM	A corm.
WHEN TO PLANT	August.
WHERE TO PLANT	In a 6-inch (15cm) pot, indoors.
HOW DEEP TO PLANT	Place corm on top of compost with its base firmly settled into the soil.
IN WHAT SORT OF SOIL	Any multi-purpose potting compost.
WHAT YOU NEED	A corm, one 6-inch (15cm) pot, multi-purpose compost, a handful of gravel, a stone.
HOW TO PLANT	Place a stone over the drainage hole and then a handful of gravel in bottom of pot. Fill with compost and firm with fingertips so that the compost lies 1 inch (2½cm) below the rim of the pot. Place corm firmly on top. 
AFTERCARE	Keep cool (10-16°C/50-61°F) throughout the rest of the summer and autumn. Keep compost moist and wait for shoots to appear. Indoor cyclamen like cool conditions and have a dormant period from spring until August. Gently pull off flowers and leaves as they turn yellow.
WATERING	Keep compost just moist during growing period. Water often when in flower, carefully and slowly making sure no water gets into the middle of the corm. Do not overwater!
FEEDING	Once a week with a liquid feed when budding and flowering.
GIFT IDEAS	A beautiful winter-flowering gift to last for years. Pretty shuttlecock-shaped flowers of red, pink or white and silver marbled leaves. Present in a wicker basket the same size as the pot.

MONEY TREE

A shoot from an existing plant — a cutting, or small bought plant with 2 or 3 pairs of leaves.

April.

In a pot, indoors.

Insert the base of the shoot into the compost.

Any multi-purpose potting compost.

A shoot, 4-inch (10cm) pot, compost, and stones or gravel.

First put a handful of stones in the bottom of the pot, followed by compost which is firmed down with the fingertips. Make sure that the compost is 1 inch (2½cm) below the rim of the pot. Insert the base of the cutting into the compost, and water thoroughly.

The shoot will soon grow its own roots and begin to develop. Repot into a pot one size larger every year or so. Keep in a warm and sunny position either outside or in during summer. Do not expose to freezing temperatures. Keep in a cool room (around 16°C/60°F) in winter. It will put up with a fair bit of neglect! Propagate further plants from leaves once the plant is fully established.

Keep compost moist from April to September, and keep compost on the dry side during winter.

Every 3 weeks with a liquid feed from April to September.

A money tree eventually grows into a bonsai-like tree, a perfect decoration for a sunny windowsill. Present in a terracotta pot with a silk flower glued onto the side.

BUSY LIZZIE

A 4-inch (10cm) cutting from an existing plant.
†Parental supervision required.

March to August.

In a pot, indoors.

Insert cutting 1 inch (2½cm) deep in compost.

Any multi-purpose compost.

One cutting, one 4-inch (10cm) pot, compost, rooting (hormone) powder, jam jar or polythene bag, small stones or gravel.

Cut a non-flowering side shoot from an existing plant, pull off its lower leaves, and stand it in water until you're ready to plant it. Put a handful of small stones or gravel in the bottom of the pot, followed by the compost which you firm down, so that the compost sits 1 inch (2½cm) from the rim of the pot. Make a small, 1 inch (2½cm) hole with a pencil or stick in the compost in the centre of the pot, dip the base of the cutting in the hormone powder, tap off the excess, and place it gently in the prepared hole.

Firm around it gently, water, and place the jam jar or plastic bag over the top. Keep it out of direct sunlight for about 2 weeks, until it has taken root. Pot it on every spring into a pot one size larger. Busy lizzies like the warm and the light, with a minimum temperature of 12°C/54°F during winter.

Keep compost moist throughout the year.

Every 2 weeks from May to September.

A welcome gift at any time of the year, indeed it is quite capable of flowering all the year round! Cover the soil surface with moss and wrap the pot in gift wrapping paper secured with ribbon and a bow.

December

PLANT/FLOWER	CHRISTMAS CACTUS
WHAT IT GROWS FROM	A leaf cutting or a small bought plant. †Parental supervision required.
WHEN TO PLANT	April.
WHERE TO PLANT	In a 4-inch (10cm) pot or hanging basket, indoors.
HOW DEEP TO PLANT	1 inch (2½cm).
IN WHAT SORT OF SOIL	Any multi-purpose compost.
WHAT YOU NEED	Cutting, pot, compost, rooting powder, jam jar or polythene bag, small stones or gravel.
HOW TO PLANT	First put a handful of small stones or gravel in the bottom of the pot, followed by the compost, which is firmed with the tips of your fingers so that the compost sits 1 inch (2½cm) below the rim of the pot. Cut off a 4-inch (10cm) cutting from an existing plant — this will comprise 2 or 3 segments. Dip the end in rooting powder, and insert it in the compost, and firm around the base. Water. Place a jam jar or polythene bag over the top. 
AFTERCARE	Keep it in a light place, but out of direct sunlight for its first 2 weeks. You will know it has taken root when it starts growing new shoots. Repot every year into a pot one size larger. Keep as cool as possible during summer.
WATERING	Allow compost to dry out between waterings.
FEEDING	Every 2 weeks, with a liquid feed, from August to October.
GIFT IDEAS	The Christmas cactus makes a wonderful gift, which will last for many years. Wrap the pot in Christmas wrapping paper secured with a ribbon and bow.

HYACINTH	CHRISTMAS ROSE
A 'prepared' bulb. Bulbs for forcing for Christmas will only flower from 'prepared' bulbs.	A small, bought plant.
Late August/early September.	October.
In a bowl, indoors.	In a 12-inch (30cm) pot, outside, or out in the garden.
Plant so that the tips of the bulbs just show above the compost.	Same depth as potted plant.
Any multi-purpose compost or 'bulb fibre'.	Any multi-purpose compost.
8-inch (20cm) bowl, 5 bulbs, compost.	One plant, pot, compost, small stones or gravel.
Fill bowl three-quarters full, place bulbs gently onto compost, add more compost around bulbs, and water thoroughly.	First put small stones or gravel to a depth of 2 inches (5cm) in the bottom of the pot, and fill with compost. Plant and firm.
Keep well watered, in a cool (not freezing) and dark place for 10 weeks, or until the shoots are about 1 inch (2½cm) high with the flower buds inside the leaves visible. For 2 weeks keep in a slightly warmer and lighter room, after which time they can be brought into the warm sitting room. Once they have faded they can be planted out in the garden.	Keep in a shady place.
Keep compost moist at all times.	Keep compost moist at all times.
Not necessary.	Liquid feed every 2 or 3 weeks during summer.
Lay moss or gravel between the bulbs and wrap a large, lush ribbon around the bowl and tie with a bow.	Christmas roses produce lovely white flowers with golden centres. They flower better in a cool greenhouse or conservatory during very cold spells in winter. Wrap the pot in a pretty piece of material and secure it with ribbon tied in a bow.

HELPFUL HINTS

HOW TO REPOT

Plants need to be repotted to give more room to their roots. Repot into pots one size larger, in the spring.

Put small stones in the bottom of the new pot and then a little multi-purpose potting compost. Remove plant from its old pot by holding it upside down and tapping the edge of the pot on something solid. Put the plant in its new pot and fill in around the edge, gently pushing the compost in with a stick. Water thoroughly. You may have to add a little more compost after the first watering in the new pot.

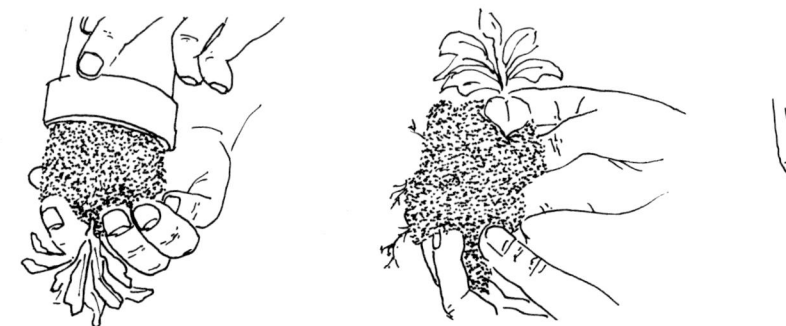

HOW TO TAKE A CUTTING

As a general rule, cuttings from soft shoots are taken in the spring. You will need: multi-purpose potting compost, 4-inch (10cm) pots, small stones, a polythene bag and a rubber band, or a jam jar.

First put a handful of small stones in the bottom of the pot and fill with potting compost, firming it, so that it is 1 inch ($2\frac{1}{2}$cm) below the rim of the pot. As in the case of the common geranium, 4-inch (10cm) side shoots are cut off at a leaf joint, and the lower leaves are pulled off. The end is then dipped in rooting powder, and inserted 1 inch ($2\frac{1}{2}$cm) into the compost. Cover with a polythene bag and secure it with the rubber band, or cover with a jam jar. Keep warm, out of direct sunlight, and remove cover two weeks later.

HELPFUL HINTS

HOW TO GROW PARSNIPS AND BRUSSELS SPROUTS FOR CHRISTMAS DAY, AS WELL AS SAGE AND ONION FOR THE STUFFING

You will need to borrow a bit of garden to grow all of these, except the sage. Dig it over well and clear out all the weeds and then let it stand for a couple of weeks before planting.

Sow **Parsnips** in March or April in furrows 1 inch (2½cm) deep, 18 inches (45cm) apart. Place seed in threes, 6 inches (15cm) apart, and later select the strongest seedling from each station. Parsnips can be harvested as and when required.

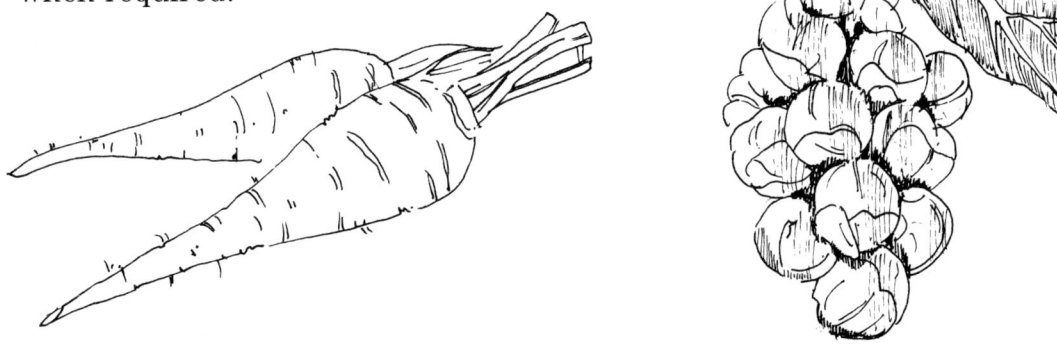

Plant **Brussels Sprouts** in March outdoors, 3 feet (1 meter) apart in a soil that has been enriched with manure. Feed with a liquid feed every 2 weeks during summer. Protect from cabbage white butterflies with fine netting. Gather sprouts starting from the bottom of the stem.

Onions are grown most easily from sets, or small onions, planted in March 6 inches (15cm) apart in rows 12 inches (30cm) apart, at soil level in the spring. Water well in dry weather, and feed every 10 days with a liquid feed during June and July. Once mature, they can be dug up and laid in the sun to dry. Then store in a cool and dry place until required.

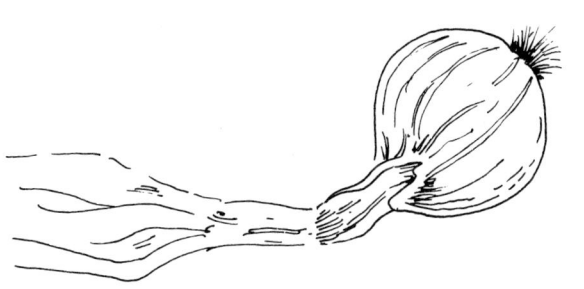

Sage is easily grown in a pot or in the ground, in a sunny place from a bought plant, or cuttings taken in the autumn. Leaves are cut and dried in July.

YOUR PERSONAL DIARY

	January	February	March	April	May	June
1						
2						
3						
4						
5						
6						
7						
8						
9						
10						
11						
12						
13						
14						
15						
16						
17						
18						
19						
20						
21						
22						
23						
24						
25						
26						
27						
28						
29						
30						
31						

YOUR PERSONAL DIARY

July	August	September	October	November	December	
						1
						2
						3
						4
						5
						6
						7
						8
						9
						10
						11
						12
						13
						14
						15
						16
						17
						18
						19
						20
						21
						22
						23
						24
						25
						26
						27
						28
						29
						30
						31

WHEN TO PLANT

January		
Witch Hazel	October
Algerian Iris	September
Begonia Rex	June

February		
Snowdrops	October
Daffodils	October to December
Clivia	April

March		
Mustard and Cress	February
African Violet	Midsummer
Prickly Cacti	April

April		
Crocus	Autumn
Primrose	March
Amaryllis	March

May		
Bluebells	Autumn
Basil (Sweet)	Early April
Coleus	February

June		
Miniature Roses	May
Sweet Peas	February/March
Geraniums	August/September

July		
Strawberries	Spring
Morning Glory	Late March/early April
Lily (Candidum)	January/February

August		
Cherry Tomatoes	March
Nasturtium	April
Rosemary	Spring or Summer

September		
Tangerine	Spring
Chinese Lanterns	March
Fuchsia	Spring

October		
Mint	September
Giant Pumpkins	May
Guernsey Lily	July to September

November		
Cyclamen	August
Money Tree	April
Busy Lizzie	March to August

December		
Christmas Cactus	April
Hyacinth	August/early September
Christmas Rose	October